Extreme Animals

Nature's Fastest Animals

Frankie Stout

PowerKiDS press

New York

For Nicholas Anthony Lazarus, a wonderful nephew

Published in 2008 by The Rosen Publishing Group, Inc.
29 East 21st Street, New York, NY 10010

First Edition

Editor: Jennifer Way
Book Design: Greg Tucker
Photo Researcher: Nicole Pristash

Photo Credits: Cover, p. 15 by Digital Vision; p. 5 © www.iStockphoto.com/Rich Phalin; pp. 7, 11 Shutterstock.com; p. 9 by Artville; p. 12–13 by Digital Stock; p. 16 © G. Delpho/Peter Arnold, Inc.; p. 18 © Doug Perrine/naturepl.com; p. 21 © S. Purdy Matthews/Getty Images.

Library of Congress Cataloging-in-Publication Data

Stout, Frankie.
  Nature's fastest animals / Frankie Stout. — 1st ed.
    p. cm. — (Extreme animals)
  Includes index.
  ISBN 978-1-4042-4156-5 (lib. bdg.)
  1. Animal locomotion—Juvenile literature. I. Title.
  QP301.S845 2008
  573.7'9—dc22
                                            2007023216

Manufactured in the United States of America

Contents

Extreme Speed

Some animals are known for their **speed**. They can move very fast to catch **prey**, to get away from danger, or just to get to where they are going.

These **extremely** fast animals come in all sizes and shapes and live in all kinds of **habitats**. Cheetahs, ostriches, antelopes, falcons, sharks, and many other animals are known for moving very quickly. The cheetah is the fastest animal on land, and the peregrine falcon is the fastest in the air. From feathered birds to hairy gnus, many animals in the natural world will shock you with their extreme speed.

The pronghorn, shown here, is one of the fastest animals in the world. It can reach speeds of up to 60 miles per hour (97 km/h). The pronghorn lives in North America.

Built for Speed

Extremely fast runners have powerful **muscles** in their thighs. Animals' bodies use these muscles to move very quickly. Some very fast runners, like greyhounds and cheetahs, are so quick that at times their feet do not touch the ground at all as they run!

Other animals do not run, but they may swim or fly very quickly. Their body is **adapted** to move around in their **environments**. For example, falcons have wings that are long and pointed. This makes it easy for them to move through the air. The same is true of an animal like a shark, whose body is shaped so it can **glide** very quickly through water.

In this picture, you can see these greyhounds at a point at which none of their feet are touching the ground while they are running.

Gnus Flash

The wildebeest, also known as the gnu, is a kind of antelope that lives in Africa. Wildebeests are some of the fastest runners on Earth. They can run up to 50 miles per hour (80 km/h)!

Wildebeests live in herds. Each herd can have as few as 20 or as many as thousands of wildebeests. Sometimes herds of wildebeests rest and eat together with herds of zebras.

Wildebeests need their speed to escape **predators**. Cheetahs, lions, hyenas, and even crocodiles all hunt and eat wildebeests. Wildebeests are big and provide a lot of meat for a predator fast enough to catch them. They can weigh as much as 500 pounds (225 kg).

The name wildebeest comes from the Afrikaans language and means "wild cattle."

Fastest on Earth

The cheetah, a member of the cat family, can run up to 70 miles per hour (113 km/h)! This is about as fast as a car on a freeway!

Cheetahs are leaner than other big cats, and they have longer legs. This helps them run faster than any other cat. In fact, cheetahs can run faster than any other land animal.

A cheetah would rather run than fight when it is in danger. It uses its speed to its own advantage to outrun larger predators. It also uses its speed to outrun and catch its prey. Cheetahs hunt **mammals** like rabbits, gazelles, and wildebeests.

The cheetah can keep up its high speed only for about 500 yards (457 m). This is because running so fast in the African heat can hurt a cheetah's body.

Cheetahs are an endangered species. This means that they are in danger of dying out forever.

The Cheetah

Cheetahs' tails are about 28 ½ inches (72 cm) long and end in a puff of white fur.

Big Cats

Adult cheetahs weigh about 100 pounds (45 kg).

Extreme Facts

1. Adult cheetahs' bodies are about 4 feet (1 m) long.

2. Newborn cheetah cubs have a thick, dark coat of fur, called a mantle, along their back.

3. When cheetahs run, only one of their feet touches the ground at any given time.

4. Cheetahs today live in the wild in Africa.

Adult cheetahs are about 30 inches (76 cm) high at the shoulder.

WOW!!

Cheetahs can **accelerate** from 0 to 70 miles per hour (0–113 km/h) in 3 seconds!

Big, Fast, and Feathered

The ostrich is the fastest bird on land. This big bird cannot fly, but it has long legs with powerful muscles that help it run fast over long distances. Ostriches can run up to 45 miles per hour (72 km/h). Ostriches have to be extremely fast to outrun predators that hunt them, such as lions.

The name ostrich comes from the Greek words meaning "camel bird." This is because ostriches have a long neck, like a camel. Ostriches are the biggest birds in the world, weighing about 250 pounds (113 kg). Some male ostriches have grown to be 9 feet (3 m) tall!

Ostriches have good eyesight and good hearing. These senses can give ostriches a head start in running away from predators!

Fast Fliers

Ostriches are the fastest birds on land, but the peregrine falcon is the world's fastest flier. A peregrine falcon generally flies at about 70 miles per hour (113 km/h). When it dives to catch its prey, it can reach speeds of up to 200 miles per hour (322 km/h)! Though they are not as fast as peregrine falcons, homing pigeons can fly at speeds of up to 94 miles per hour (151 km/h) for long periods of time.

Some bugs can also fly very fast. There are dragonflies that can fly as fast as 60 miles per hour (97 km/h)!

It is thought that peregrine falcons have a special nose that helps slow the wind that rushes in when the falcon enters a dive. If it did not have this special nose, too much air would be forced into the lungs and make them burst!

Lightning-Fast Swimmers

Fish and sea mammals get around by swimming. Some fish, like the tuna, use their powerful body to swim quickly and catch their meals. Others, like the mako shark, have a long, narrow body that is adapted to move through water with lightning speed.

The world's fastest fish is the cosmopolitan sailfish. It can swim up to 68 miles per hour (109 km/h). However, like the cheetah, the sailfish can keep up its extreme speed only for short distances. Moving very quickly can make an animal very tired.

The sailfish, shown here, is a lightning-fast swimmer. It is also known for the huge jumps it can make up into the air.

Fast Living

All kinds of animals use their body to run, swim, and fly around at great speeds. Some animals use their extreme speed to hunt. Other animals can escape danger by running away from it quickly. Extreme speed can even help an animal catch its meal one day and help it escape being eaten on another day!

Extreme speed can be a great **benefit** to animals, both big and small, in air, on land, and in the water. Extreme speed helps animals live in their habitats.

Lions and zebras are both fast and can run at around the same speeds. Winning a race is not a game for wild animals, it is a matter of life and death!

Fast Facts

Fastest animal on land: A cheetah can run 70 miles per hour (113 km/h).

Fastest animal in air: Peregrine falcons can dive at 200 miles per hour (322 km/h).

Fastest animal in water: A cosmopolitan sailfish can swim 68 miles per hour (109 km/h).

Fastest mammal in water: A common dolphin can swim 64 miles per hour (103 km/h).

Fastest human: The world record speed for a human is 28 miles per hour (45 km/h).

Fastest bug: Dragonflies can speed around at up to 60 miles per hour (97 km/h).

Glossary

accelerate (ik-SEH-luh-rayt) To go faster.

adapted (uh-DAPT-ed) Changed to fit requirements.

benefit (BEH-neh-fit) To do well because of something.

environments (en-VY-ern-ments) All the living things of places.

extremely (ek-STREEM-lee) Very.

glide (GLYD) To fall freely through the air without flying.

habitats (HA-beh-tats) The kinds of land where animals or plants naturally live.

mammals (MA-mulz) Animals that have a backbone and hair, breathe air, and feed milk to their young.

muscles (MUH-sulz) Parts of the body that make the body move.

predators (PREH-duh-terz) Animals that kill other animals for food.

prey (PRAY) An animal that is hunted by another animal for food.

speed (SPEED) How fast something goes.

Index

Web Sites

Due to the changing nature of Internet links, PowerKids Press has developed an online list of Web sites related to the subject of this book. This site is updated regularly. Please use this link to access the list:
www.powerkidslinks.com/exan/fast/